ARTIFICIAL INTELLIGENCE ART
and Other Creative Tech

Co-published by agreement between Shi Tu Hui and World Book, Inc.

Shi Tu Hui
Room 1807, Block 1,
#3 West Dawang Road
Chaoyang District, Beijing 100025
P.R. China

World Book, Inc
180 North LaSalle Street
Suite 900
Chicago, Illinois 60601
USA

Library of Congress Cataloging-in-Publication Data for this volume has been applied for.

Cool Tech (set #2)
ISBN: 978-0-7166-5387-5 (set, hc)

Artificial Intelligence Art and Other Creative Tech
ISBN: 978-0-7166-5389-9 (hc)

Also available as:
ISBN: 978-0-7166-5395-0 (e-book)
ISBN: 978-0-7166-5401-8 (soft cover)

Written by Alex Woolf

STAFF

VP, Editorial: Tom Evans

Manager, New Product: Nicholas Kilzer

Curriculum Designer: Caroline Davidson

Proofreader: Nathalie Strassheim

Coordinator, Design Development & Production:
  Brenda Tropinski

Senior Media Editor: Rosalia Bledsoe

Developed with World Book by
White-Thomson Publishing LTD
www.wtpub.co.uk

ACKNOWLEDGMENTS

Cover   © 3Dsculptor/Shutterstock
   5   © Peepo/iStock
  6-7   © Iryna Imago, Shutterstock; © Emmanuel Lattes, Alamy Images
  8-9   © Shutterstock; © Morten Grønning, Happaratus
10-11   © Sabena Jane Blackbird, Alamy Images; © Guy Bell, Alamy Images; © MangKangMangMee/Shutterstock; © Malcolm Park, Alamy Images
12-13   2015, Mike Tyka (www.miketyka.com); Public Domain (Edmond de Belamy, from *La Famille de Belamy* GAN (2018), print on canvas published by Obvious Art); Public Domain (Encik Tekateki via DALL-E)
14-15   © Shutterstock; *Théâtre D'opéra Spatial,* Jason Allen
16-17   © Kovtun Dmitriy, Shutterstock; © Stratos Instruments
18-19   © Shutterstock; © Anthony Brown, Adobe Stock; © Matthias Oesterle, ZUMA Wire/Alamy Images
20-21   © Shutterstock; © Valente Rosas, GDA/AP Images

22-23   © Shutterstock
24-25   © Shutterstock; © SIPA Asia/ZUMA Wire/Alamy Images; © Alessandro Bosio, Pacific Press/Alamy Images
26-31   © Shutterstock
32-33   © Shutterstock; © Aleksey Popov, Dreamstime
34-35   © Shutterstock
36-37   © Alex Yuzhakov, Shutterstock; Public Domain (Robert Elliott); © Peter Nicholls, Reuters/Alamy Images; © Industrial Light & Magic
38-39   © Cavan Images/Alamy Images; © Supamotionstock.com/Shutterstock; © Yoshio Tsunoda, AFLO/Alamy Images; © 20th Century Fox
40-41   © Shutterstock
42-43   © Shutterstock; © Warner Bros.
44-45   © CJ CGV; © Dirk Waem, Belga News Agency/Alamy Images; © Sergey Nivens, Shutterstock; © Wu Hong, EPA-EFE/Shutterstock

CONTENTS

There is a glossary of terms on the first page. Terms defined
in the glossary are in boldface type that **looks like this** on
their first appearance on any spread (two facing pages).

GLOSSARY

app short for software application. A software application is a computer program that enables a human user to perform some task or activity.

audiobook a recording of a book or other piece of writing made for distribution to the public. Audiobooks are recorded on electronic files that can be downloaded onto a computer, smartphone, or another device.

copyright a collection of rights granted to artists, authors, musicians, and other creators of original works. Copyright laws seek to ensure that creative people benefit from their own creations.

digital technology all types of electronic equipment and applications that use information in the form of numeric code.

drone an uncrewed aerial vehicle. Most drones are piloted by remote control.

5G stands for fifth-generation technology. It is the most advanced standard for wireless mobile communication devices.

green screen in film and television, a green background in front of which actors are filmed. This allows a custom-designed background to be added to a scene.

haptic technology that can create an experience of touch through forces, vibrations, or motions to a user.

holography a method for electronically storing and displaying a three-dimensional image. The image created is called a hologram.

a device that produces a narrow and intense beam of light of only one wavelength going in one direction. The special qualities of laser light make it ideal for a variety of applications.

LED light-emitting diode. A tiny device that gives off light in response to an electric current. Many modern electronic devices make use of LED's.

machine learning the use of computer systems that are able to learn and adapt to new situations without following prewritten instructions.

neuron one of the cells of which the brain, spinal cord, and nerves are composed.

plagiarism the act of presenting another person's work or ideas as one's own. For example, a student who copies words or ideas from a website or book without identifying the source has committed plagiarism.

program instructions that a computer can carry out. Such instructions are generally written using computer languages or programming languages.

streaming a system for sending or receiving films, television shows, pictures, and video media over the internet.

stylus a pointed instrument used for writing. An electrically conductive stylus is used to write on or manipulate objects on a computer tablet or screen.

virtual reality also known as VR, is an artificial, three-dimensional computer environment. A VR experience is typically viewed through a headset. It replaces what a person normally sees and hears with computer-generated images and sounds.

INTRODUCTION

Would you visit an art gallery to see a painting created by a computer? Or go to a concert to listen to a symphony composed by a machine? Would you read a poem written by a software **program?** We may soon be faced with such choices. Computers and other technologies are already playing a major role in the creative arts, and this is only going to increase in the future.

Some of these technologies are simply tools to make the creative process easier or more efficient. For example, digital art software allows artists to create paintings directly on a computer. Musicians can play multiple instruments on a single digital device. Authors can write a novel using a computer program that will edit their work and even help them with their research. And filmmakers regularly use computers to design props and print them on 3D (three-dimensional) printers.

Artificial intelligence (AI) programs take the role of technology a step further. Artificial intelligence is the ability of a computer system to process information like human thought or to exhibit humanlike behavior. These aren't simply tools but collaborators in the artistic process. They work alongside human artists, contributing ideas and inspiring new forms of creative expression.

Some AI programs are artists in their own right, creating original works of art, music, and literature with no human input whatsoever. This book looks at the many ways AI technology is shaping the arts and explores how this might continue in the future.

1 ART

WHO CARES WHO MADE IT?

Imagine you can display a **holographic** light sculpture on your coffee table. It may have been made by a human artist or an artificial one, or possibly a collaboration between the two. You don't mind—what matters is that it looks great! And when you get tired of it, you can always change it for another with a touch on your phone or a spoken command. Or if you wish to have a solid sculpture, you can print one out from an image on the internet using your 3D printer.

This might seem like a scenario from science fiction. But these technologies are available today. The way art is created and consumed is changing thanks to advances in computing, materials technology, light manipulation, 3D printing, and artificial intelligence. Inevitably, this will change our perceptions of what art is and what art can be. It also challenges our views about who can create it. If a computer program creates a beautiful painting or sculpture, does that make it any less impressive?

DIGITAL ART

Digital art is any art made using **digital technology.** It began in 1963 when American computer scientist Ivan Sutherland developed Sketchpad, a program that enabled users to draw on a screen using a light-sensitive wand known as a light pen. In the mid-1980's, digital art took off with the arrival of the personal computer and programs that anyone could use. Today, advances in technology have allowed digital artists to produce evermore sophisticated work.

Digital painting. In place of a canvas, the digital artist uses a graphics tablet. Instead of a paintbrush, they use a **stylus** or even their finger. The screen of the graphics tablet is pressure sensitive, so the artist can vary the intensity of each stroke. They can choose from a palette containing millions of colors and from a wide variety of styles including oils, watercolors, pastels, charcoal, or airbrushing.

Special effects. Digital paintings are created in layers that can be edited individually. This allows artists the freedom to experiment. Any element can be removed or altered without affecting the rest of the painting. Artists can produce effects that are difficult to achieve with traditional painting, such as repeating elements or symmetrical and transparent elements. Digital painting is mess-free, and artists can paint anywhere without the need to bring a lot of equipment.

Digital sculptors first design their 3D artworks on the flat screen of a computer, using such software as ZBrush or Blender. They start with a ball of virtual clay on the screen and use a mouse or a pressure-sensitive tablet and stylus to manipulate it into the desired shape. Some use a **haptic** device, a glove that allows them to "feel" the sculpture while working on it.

From screen to reality. Some digital sculptures are output as digital files. These can be used for animation, video games, or **virtual reality.** If digital sculptors wish to turn their designs into solid objects, they can use 3D printing. The computer sends a digital file of the sculpture to the 3D printer. The printer then assembles the sculpture layer by layer, using such materials as resin, plastic, and graphite.

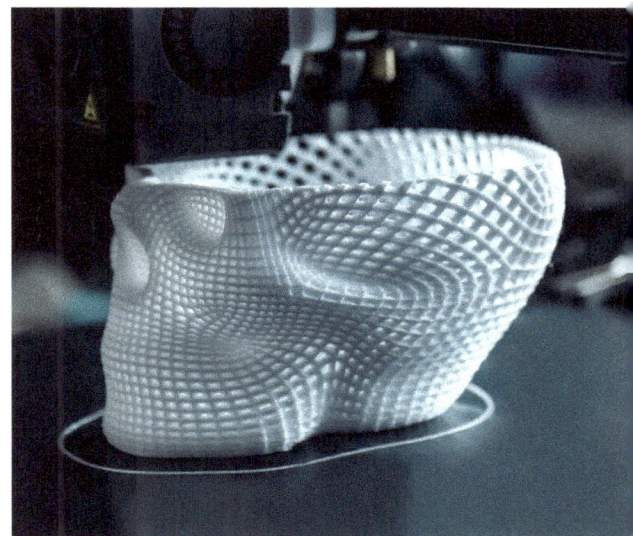

3D printing is already proving useful in a variety of applications and industries. The printers can produce objects small or large to meet almost any design and engineering need. Some 3D printed objects may even be used in the human body!

AI ARTISTS

So far, we have looked at ways computers can assist artists in their work, but computers can also be artists in their own right. Today, AI programs can generate original and unique artworks with little or no human involvement.

Algorithmic art. A computer scientist builds an AI program by creating an *algorithm* (a set of rules written in a code the computer can understand). In the case of an AI program designed to create art, the algorithm may contain rules to help it analyze thousands of human-made artworks. These rules enable the program to distinguish the various elements that make up the images, such as style, special effects, and particular forms, shapes, and patterns. The algorithm can then use this data to produce new works. One form of algorithmic art is *fractal art.* Fractals are geometric shapes in which similar patterns appear at ever-smaller scales. Algorithms can output random variations of fractals in different patterns and colors to create extraordinary pieces of abstract art.

Neural networks (NN) are AI programs inspired by the workings of the human brain. The artificial **neurons** of a NN weigh each element of an artwork and assign it a value. The value is greater if the NN encounters the element more often. If an element receives a sufficient value, the NN signals all artificial neurons connected to it. The NN often gets it wrong and attaches too much significance to an element, or not enough. The more images the NN analyzes, the more accurate it becomes. This is how it "learns."

The robot artist. Completed in 2019, Ai-Da is a humanoid robot artist who can make drawings, paintings, and sculptures. She has cameras for her eyes. Algorithms convert the visual data into instructions sent to her robot arm, allowing her to create artworks from sight.

AI ART TAKES FLIGHT

Today, AI art is gaining the respect of the art world. Machine-created artworks appear on the walls of art galleries and museums. They are found on books and music album covers and are even sold at auction. AI art is also becoming popular among nonartists, who can generate their own unique works of algorithmic art using an **app** on their phone.

Generative adversarial networks. In 2014, a team of computer scientists developed a new type of AI program called a generative adversarial network (GAN). Here, two neural networks compete against each other. One of them, the generator, analyzes a set of human-created paintings and outputs a piece of artwork. The other neural network, the discriminator, tries to distinguish the AI-generated artwork from the human art. Each NN learns from the process, so the generator gets better at imitating human-created art while the discriminator becomes more adept at spotting differences.

Mike Tyka is an artist and scientist who pioneered the use of GAN's in art. In his series, *Inceptionism,* he fed an image into a neural network and asked it to enhance whatever it saw. The NN generated a new image, and the process repeated. For example, if the NN saw a cloud that looked like a bird, then it would create similar images. Each successive image would look more birdlike. Eventually, this generated a highly detailed image of a bird from the program's own "imagination."

AI art sells. In 2018, Christie's became the first auction house to offer a work of art created by a machine. The painting, titled *Portrait of Edmond de Belamy*, sold for $432,500, more than 40 times the estimated selling price. The team behind the painting, named Obvious, fed their computer 15,000 portraits painted between the 14th century and the 20th century. They used a GAN to produce an original artwork. The resulting painting is a fascinating mixture of portrait styles from different centuries.

Text-to-art. One popular way of creating AI art is by using a text-to-image app. Users describe what they want in words, and the program generates an image matching that description. The app uses two kinds of **machine-learning** technology: an algorithm to interpret text and a neural network to generate images. Both can learn from previous attempts, and each request will generate a unique image.

An image generated by the AI program DALL-E 2 based on the text prompt "1960's art of cow getting abducted by UFO in the Midwest."

THE ETHICS OF AI ART

The rise of AI art poses some difficult ethical questions. For example, is AI art really art if it's not created by a conscious being? Is it okay for AI artists to put human artists out of work? And should AI artists be allowed to mimic the styles of human artists? Is this not an infringement of human artists' copyright?

Is it art? AI artists are not "aware" in the human sense that they are creating art, they are simply following a set of instructions in an algorithm. For some, this suggests they are not creating art. According to the British children's illustrator Rob Biddulph, "True art is about the creative process much more than it's about the final piece. And simply pressing a button to generate an image is not a creative process."

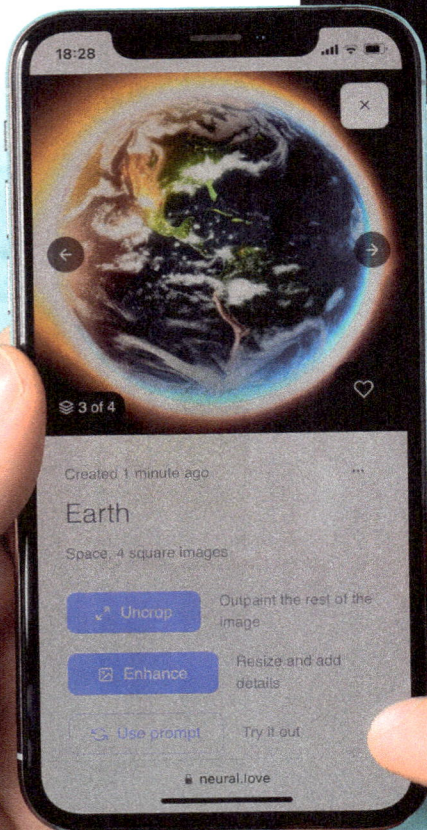

Copyright. Many illustrators are unhappy that AI image generators make free use of their **copyrighted** artwork without giving them any credit. The algorithms learn from these images and generate new images in the same style. Thus, human illustrators are essentially helping to train AI artists for no reward. Of course, human artists often imitate the styles of other artists. But they usually bring something of themselves to the work. Perhaps the AI programmers need to demonstrate that they are doing the same.

HUMAN VS. AI

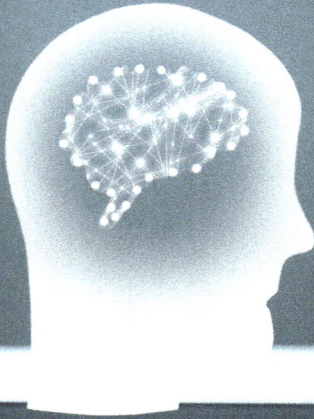

Threatened livelihoods. Many illustrators worry that their clients will opt for cheap AI-generated artwork, making it harder for them to earn a living from their craft. They fear that AI art devalues illustration because traditional skills and experience will no longer count for anything.

The role of the artist. In 2022, game designer Jason M. Allen won first prize in the digital arts category at the Colorado State Fair Fine Arts competition. He used an AI art generator named Midjourney to create his image, titled *Théâtre d'Opéra Spatial*. Midjourney produces images from written prompts. Several artists believed his artwork ought to be disqualified because it was created by a machine. Allen argued that the art involved plenty of effort on his part. He altered his written prompt many times to create 900 versions of the image before he was satisfied. This raises questions about the role of the artist when working with AI. We may have to adjust our views about this as these technologies continue to advance.

2 MUSIC

PROGRAMMED PLAYLISTS AND PERFORMANCES

Today, we live in a world where music is available at the touch of a button. We can curate our playlists to suit our mood—whether it's to inspire us to greater efforts while exercising or something to help wind down after a stressful day. **Streaming** services employ algorithms that help us find songs to our taste among the millions available. The latest speaker technology ensures excellent sound quality when we listen.

Technology hasn't only revolutionized how we consume music but also how it is produced and performed. AI programs can assist human composers, and some can even generate their own original music. Computers can precisely imitate the timbre of any instrument or produce completely new sounds. In some cases, musicians don't even need to perform—holographic copies can take their place on stage.

The invention of the piano in the early 1700's and the electric guitar in the 1930's inspired musicians to make new kinds of music. That process continues to this day. The arrival of computers has again transformed music making, helping composers develop ideas and produce recordings, and offering them new creative tools and techniques.

Digital audio workstations (DAW's) are electronic systems that allow musicians to compose, arrange, record, edit, and mix music in their homes, avoiding the need for a recording studio. Most DAW's consist of a computer and an audio interface that provides audio signals to and from the computer. They also include audio editing software and such input devices as a MIDI (Musical Instrument Digital Interface)—a keyboard, microphone, and a set of speakers. DAW's in the future will include software that suggests ways to improve sound quality and *dynamics* (varying volume levels of different elements), simplifying the job of the audio engineer.

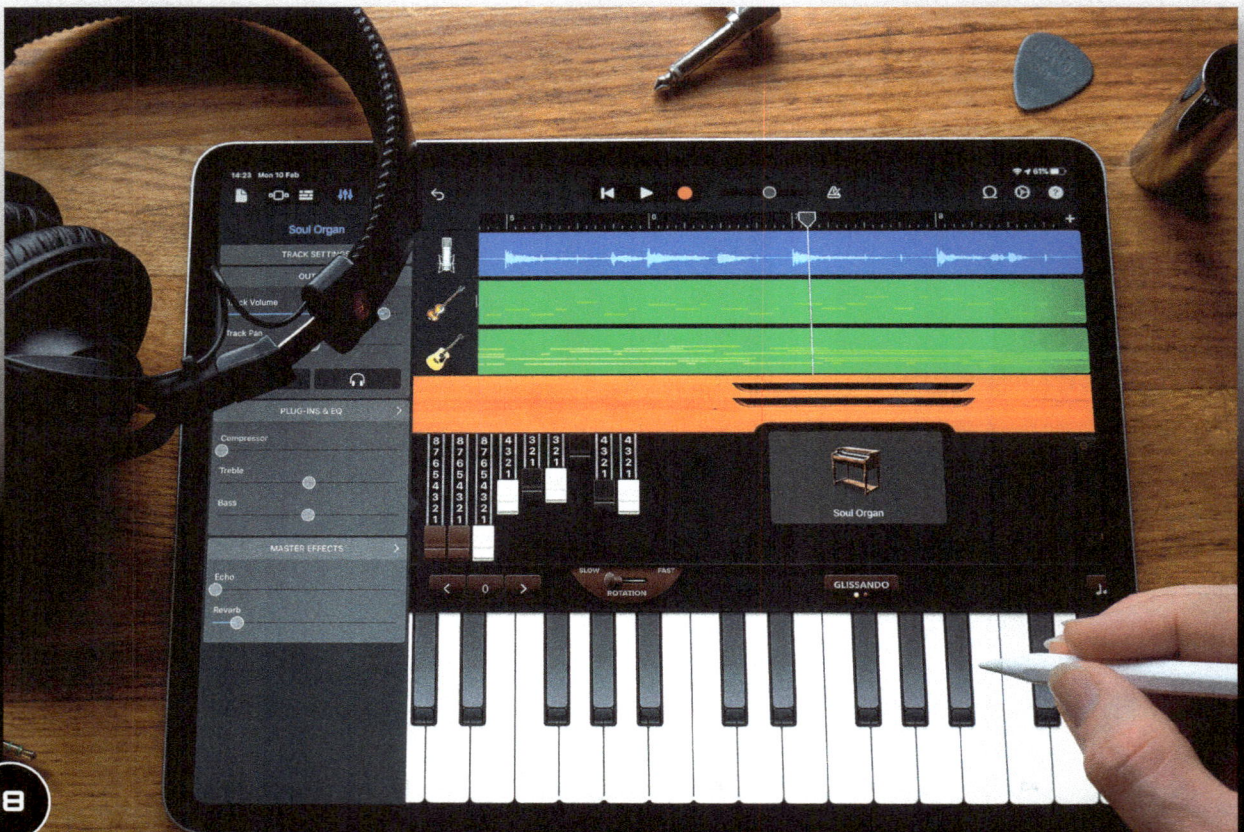

Virtual instruments. Virtual instrument software programs generate the sounds of real instruments, such as pianos, violins, or trumpets. The sounds can then be played via a MIDI keyboard connected to a DAW. These sounds are set to become even more authentic. A team of researchers named Next Generation Sound Synthesis (NESS) has developed software that synthesizes the precise sounds of instruments. The program can replicate the changing air pressure in a trumpet, the sound of fingers on a guitar fretboard, or the friction of a bow on a violin.

Composers will soon be able to choose combinations of sounds from different instruments. An AI research team named Google Magenta has fed notes from hundreds of different instruments into a neural network. The NN analyzes the sounds and blends them, creating new sounds never heard before.

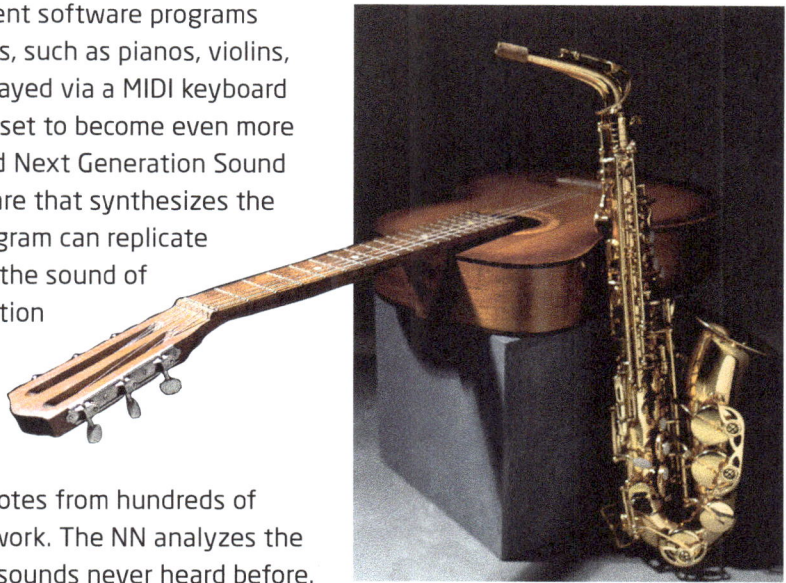

Enhancing traditional instruments.
The magnetic resonator piano is a traditional acoustic piano with a difference. Electromagnets added to each string cause them to vibrate independently of the hammers. This allows the pianist to control the volume, length, and timbre of each note they play after they have touched the key.

New instruments. Composers are also making use of newly invented musical instruments, including the optron—a tube containing colorful lights and electronics that is played like a guitar. Sensors on its surface generate music depending on where the musician places their fingers and the amount of pressure applied. Waving and tilting the optron creates other sounds and light effects. The **laser** harp is a grid of laser beams attached to a computer. The player moves their hand through the beams, and the computer turns this into sounds.

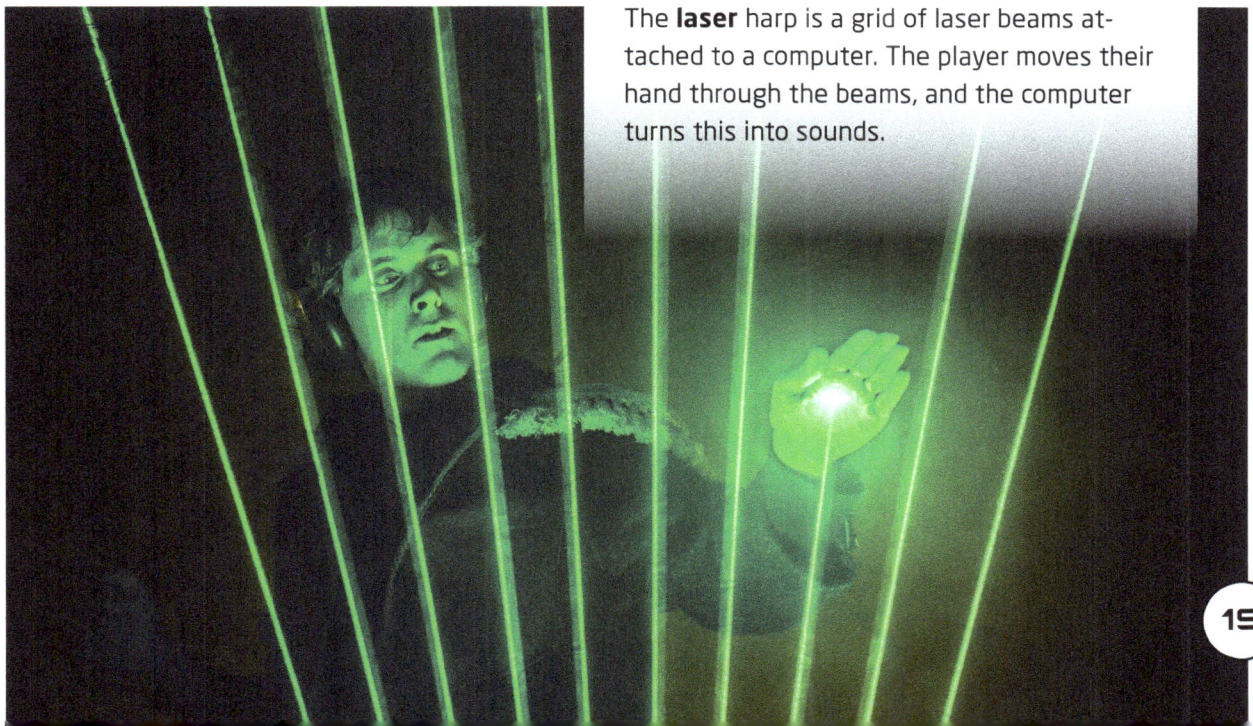

PERFORMING MUSIC

Imagine being able to stream your favorite song, and the singer performs it for you in the form of a hologram. Imagine musicians on different continents playing live on stage together. Technology is transforming our experience of musical performance, making it more personalized, more immersive, and more spectacular.

Concerts. Musicians are using cutting-edge technology to enhance stage performances. Gesture armbands allow performers to control sound and stage lighting by waving their arms. The armbands measure electrical activity in the wearer's muscles and transmit the signals via Bluetooth to devices on the stage. Tone sculptor gloves can create sounds using hand motions. Using motion-tracking technology, they translate hand motions into signals for musical control. Xylobands are radio-controlled **LED** wristbands worn by audience members. They create multiple flash patterns, making the audience part of the light show at concerts.

Live collaboration. The powerful connectivity of **5G** is making it possible for artists living in separate places to play together live on the same stage. Musicians in London, Sydney, and Los Angeles can rehearse and perform together, seeing and interacting with each other and keeping in perfect time. Such collaboration was impossible in the past due to connectivity problems using the internet.

Holographic performers. Today, we can see concerts by performers who are no longer with us. 3D versions of the musicians appear to sing and dance on stage as they did at the height of their fame. To create these performances, look-alike actors are filmed using motion-capture technology and computer-generated imagery in front of a **green screen.** This video is projected onto a transparent reflective surface to create the "hologram." It's not a true hologram because the image flattens out up close. Real holograms are 3D images created by interference of light beams that can be viewed from all angles and up close. However, audiences are far enough away from the stage that they see realistic 3D simulations of their idols.

Personalized performances. Soon, it may be possible to connect a concert venue's soundboard to a phone app. Audience members using headphones can then choose to set their own sound mix—honing in on particular instruments or microphones on stage. They will be able to do the same with video, choosing their preferred perspective from multiple camera angles, streaming and sharing their photos and videos live from the concert.

AI-ASSISTED MUSIC

Artificial intelligence (AI) is changing the way music is created and heard. It is making the production process more efficient for songwriters, sound engineers, and the industry as a whole, and helping fans find the music they like. Whether this will lead to improved creativity is open to question. It may end up creating music that all sounds the same.

Helping songwriters. Sometimes songwriters are stuck for inspiration. They know the style of song they want to compose but can't think of a melody. Apps like Amadeus Code can offer suggestions to kick-start their imagination. The user inputs a list of songs they like, and the app generates new melodies and chords based on the particular era and genre of those songs.

Mixing and mastering. A sound mixer combines sounds in a multitrack recording and balances the volume, richness, depth, and other qualities. Mastering puts the final touches on a sound mix by adjusting levels for consistency and removing any clicks and pops to create a polished, clean sound. AI algorithms automate these tasks. The user uploads a track and specifies the genre and style to guide the algorithm, which analyzes the track and applies the necessary changes. However, many musicians believe there is an art to mixing and mastering that cannot be replicated by a machine. They want to continue using human sound engineers.

Streaming recommendations.
AI is extremely good at spotting patterns in large amounts of data. Algorithms can analyze the listening patterns of millions of people on streaming platforms and use this to make recommendations and create playlists for individual users.

Predicting the next hit. With so many songs being released, how does the music industry discover promising new artists? AI can help here. By analyzing thousands of hit songs, programs such as Musiio learn what characteristics tend to be popular with the listening public. These filters can comb through new songs and predict future hits. The risk from this approach, of course, is that songs could begin to sound quite similar.

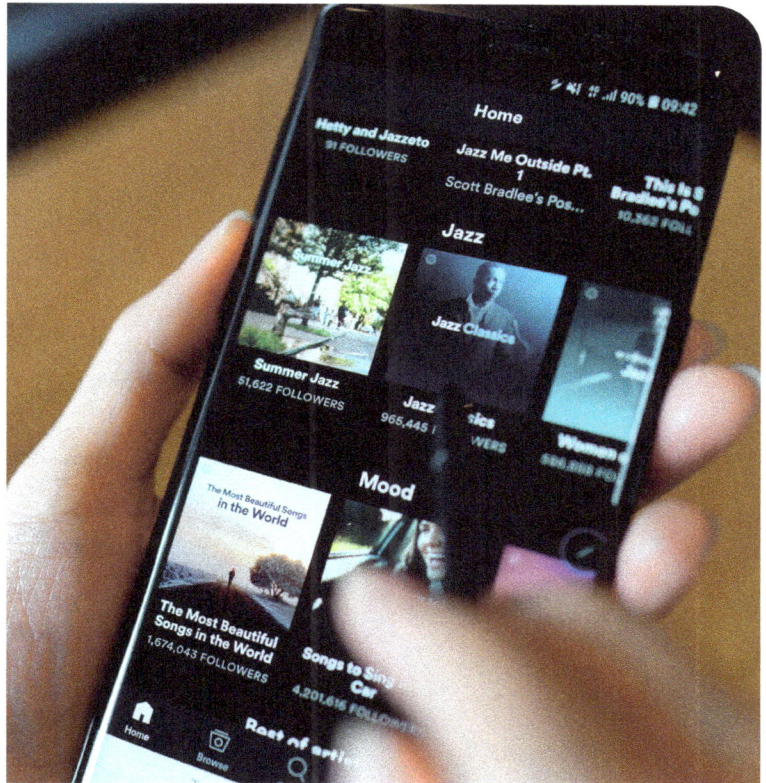

AI COMPOSERS

AI researchers are taking the next step and creating algorithms that can compose original music. Musicians are divided about where this will lead. Some dismiss the idea that machines can produce anything truly inventive or original. Others believe that collaboration with AI could spur them to new heights of musical creativity.

Mimicry and improvisation. AI programs can be fed dozens of songs by a certain composer or band and produce original music that sounds very similar. This AI mimicry has been used to create new songs, including the Beatles-like "Daddy's Car." These songs have their own unique structure, musical phrases, and melodies. Yet they still manage to sound unnervingly like the original bands. A London-based team named Bronze has created an AI program that takes human-composed songs and improvises with them in unpredictable ways. Arca, a Venezuela-born musician who has worked with Bronze, describes the process as "creating an ecosystem where things tend to happen, but never in the order you were imagining them."

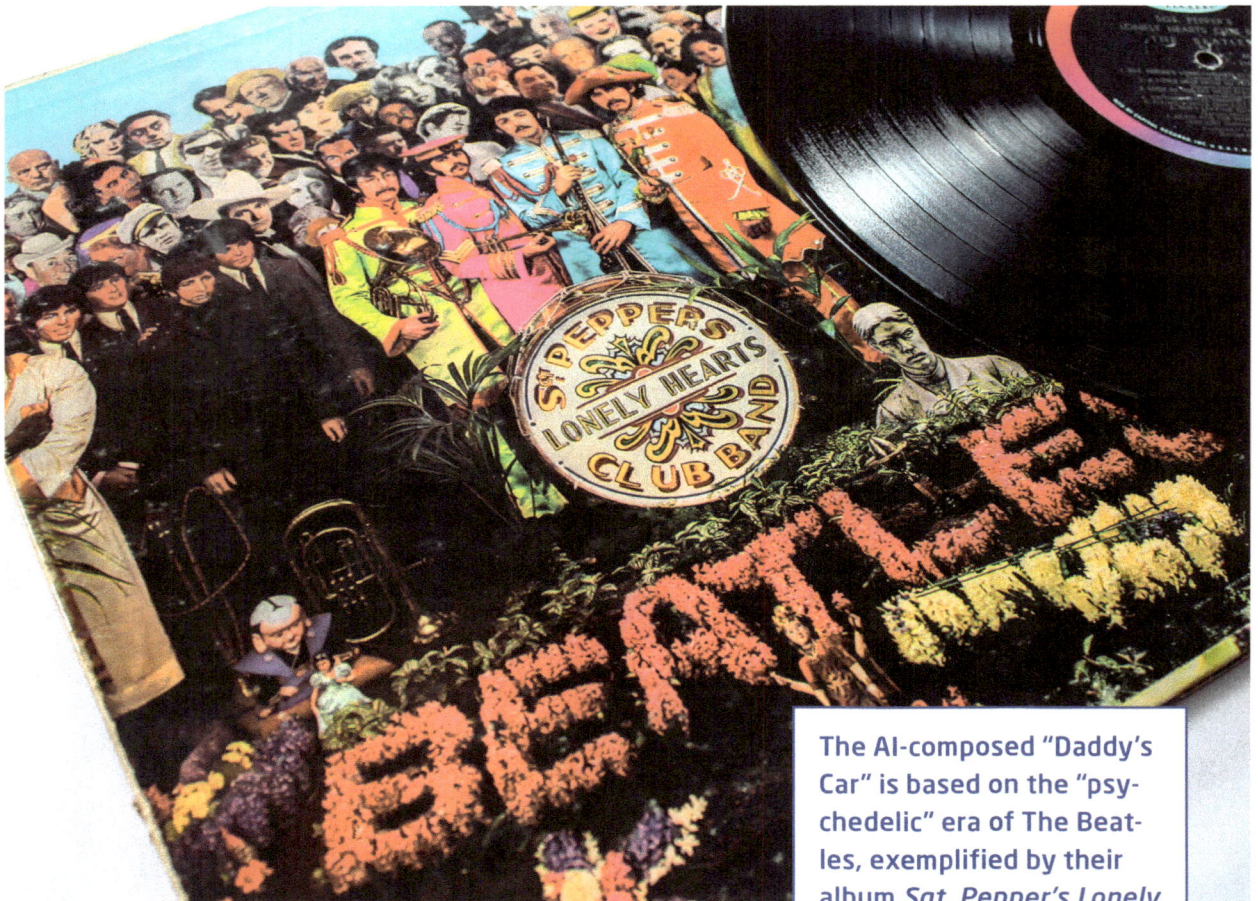

The AI-composed "Daddy's Car" is based on the "psychedelic" era of The Beatles, exemplified by their album *Sgt. Pepper's Lonely Hearts Club Band*.

Original compositions. No AI program has yet been able to compose a piece that critics would laud as "great music," yet AI-created tracks are already being sold commercially. An AI named AIVA composes classical music soundtracks for movies, advertisements, and video games. AIVA uses neural networks to recognize patterns and learn music theory from a large database of classical music. When composing, it is not given explicit instructions but finds its way within the constraints of music theory to generate its music.

Collaboration and accompaniment. Many see exciting potential for AI programs as musical collaborators, both as composers and performers. Interesting collaborations are already happening. In 2019, on her album *Proto*, singer-songwriter Holly Herndon harmonized with an AI version of herself. With their album *Chain Tripping*, the dance-pop band YACHT fed an AI music generator their back catalog. It generated a few thousand ideas—melodic fragments of between two and 16 bars—which became the source material for new songs.

Personalized soundscapes. A music-composing app named Endel designs real-time, personalized soundscapes for listeners. It takes into account the weather, the listener's heart rate, and their sleep-wake cycle, and generates music to suit their mood.

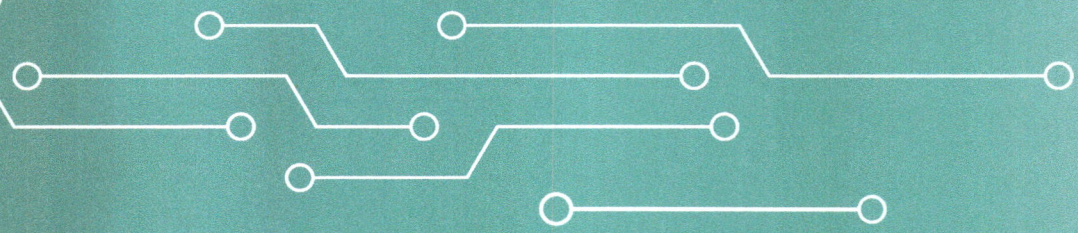

3 WRITING

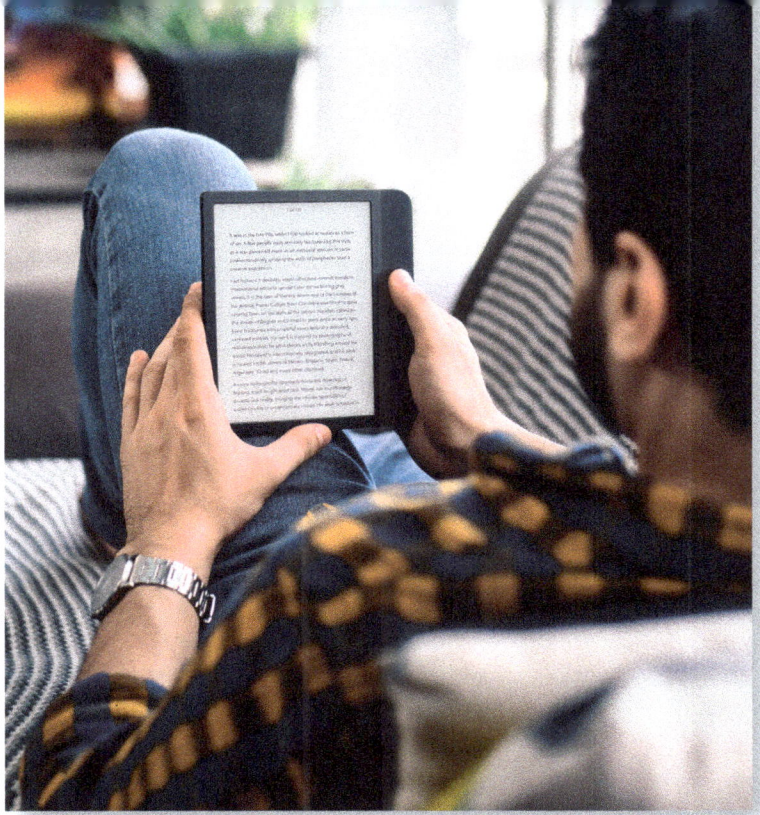

AI FOR AUTHORS

Imagine listening to an **audiobook** written by a computer and narrated by a computer-generated voice. That day may not be very far off. Today, we still live in a world of mainly human writers, but the role of machines as intelligent writing assistants is steadily increasing. The latest word-processing software doesn't only check spelling and grammar, it can offer advice on vocabulary and tone. Writers can harness the power of AI to help them research a book or give them writing tips.

AI programs excel at understanding and imitating human speech, so writers no longer need to use a keyboard to tell their stories. They can create audiobooks from their works without the need for a human narrator. Machines could soon be writing books themselves. They are already capable of generating clear, well-structured text on virtually any subject. Companies are using them to write articles, advertisements, emails, and blog posts. You may have read one yourself without realizing it.

HELPING AUTHORS

Writing has been getting steadily easier over the decades thanks to technology. In 1827, the fountain pen was invented, and writers no longer needed to recharge their pens in an inkwell. Forty years later, the first practical typewriter was built. In the 1970's, word-processing programs were developed for personal computers, enabling writers to edit and format their text on a screen before printing it out. Today's writers enjoy evermore sophisticated word-processing software as well as assistance from AI writing tools.

Modern word-processing programs like Scrivener offer templates for novels, nonfiction books, and screenplays. The programs help authors organize chapters, drafts, outlines, notes, and research. Such online, web-based word processors as Google Docs allow writers to edit documents and collaborate with publishers, editors, and coauthors, in real time.

AI to improve writing. Grammarly is a writing tool that employs AI to analyze text at the level of sentences and look for ways to improve it. The AI can correct tenses and suggest stronger synonyms and clearer sentence structure. Each time a user rejects one of its suggestions, Grammarly learns from this and does better next time. It recognizes tone and context and adjusts its suggestions depending on whether the writing is formal or casual.

AI for writer's block. Authors often need help getting started on an article or book. AI programs can help. With Jasper, the user inputs a few keywords and the theme, and the AI will generate a paragraph that the writer can mold to their liking. Another tool, Sudowrite, analyzes a sample of the author's manuscript and can generate hundreds of words of new text in the author's voice. It can offer a descriptive passage based on a highlighted noun, help expand scenes that feel too rushed, and suggest character secrets and plot twists.

Speech-to-text and text-to-speech. There are many voice recognition apps available, supporting most of the world's most popular languages. This is good news for writers who can use it for brainstorming ideas, dictating notes while they are out and about, and transcribing interviews. For those who prefer talking to typing, it has become a valuable writing tool.

AI-generated voices are used widely today for audio versions of books and articles. The AI analyzes thousands of hours of recordings from human voice actors and teaches itself the nuances and intonations of human speech. These computer-generated voices pause and breathe in the right places, and can adjust their volume, depth, accent, or emotion as required. Many listeners are fooled into thinking they are listening to a human.

AI AND WRITING

AI programs are assisting writers in every aspect of their work. But can machines actually produce high-quality original text themselves? The answer is yes, they can. In some kinds of writing, their work is now indistinguishable from that of humans. However, machines still struggle to replicate the more artistic forms of writing, such as novels and poetry.

AI content generators such as Jasper and ChatGPT can now produce text that is as well-crafted as that of professional writers. They can generate text quickly and cheaply, and businesses are increasingly turning to these tools to create marketing copy, blog posts, emails, and financial reports. ChatGPT can supply jokes and simple children's stories, and offer natural-sounding responses to questions on almost any topic, from celebrities to quantum mechanics.

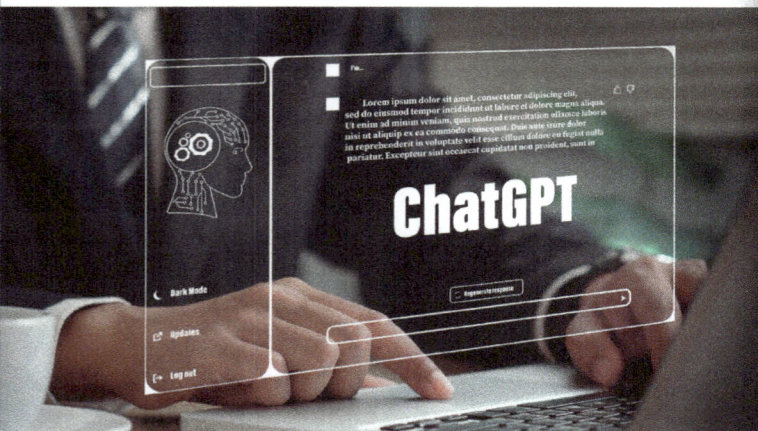

A CHAT WITH ChatGPT

Why do you write?
As an AI language model, I write to generate humanlike text based on the input I receive. My main purpose is to assist users in generating coherent, informative, and contextually relevant responses to their questions or prompts.

Have you ever tried writing a poem?
Yes ... I can generate poems based on a prompt... However, it is important to note that while I can produce text that resembles a poem, it lacks the creativity, emotions, and personal experiences that are often inherent in human-written poetry.

Do you have a favorite writer?
... I don't have personal preferences or feelings. My creators at OpenAI trained me on a diverse range of text, including the works of many famous writers ... but I don't have the ability to have a personal favorite.

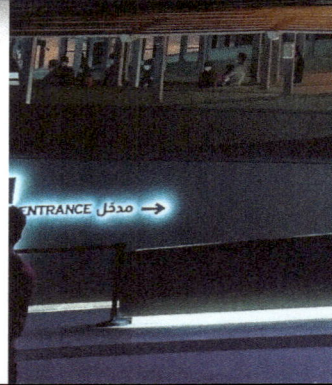

AI-writing detection. The impressive quality of AI-generated writing has tempted some unscrupulous writers to claim it as their own work. AI tools are being developed to detect AI-assisted writing and expose the cheaters. AI writing works by predicting the next likely word in a sentence. Thus, AI-generated text is more likely to use such common words as "the," "is," and "it." Human text tends to be more variable in style and vocabulary and usually contains typos. However, there is no foolproof method of detecting AI text, and this problem is likely to persist.

Writing a novel. Today, an AI could write a very simple novel with a predictable plot, straightforward characters, and familiar forms of drama. The problem, as with all forms of AI, is that machines lack the human experiences, imagination, and emotional awareness to create a story with characters that will resonate with readers. The stories they produce may be superficially entertaining but will feel similar to stories we've read before.

Writing poetry. In 2021, an AI was fed lines from more than a hundred contemporary British poets, then given some seed words and asked to compose couplets in a poetic style. Experts read through the output and selected those that most impressed them. Tracy Guiry, of the British Poetry Archive, said: "The AI would produce something that made you think. It wouldn't produce ... what a human would write because that's an incredibly subjective response; the lived experience was perhaps not there."

PUBLISHING AND READING

Technology has changed the way books are published and read just as it has changed how books are written. While print books remain highly popular, a substantial number of books are now being read in digital form on phones, tablets, and e-readers, or listened to via audiobook platforms. Publishers are responding to this demand by producing more cellular friendly and audio content.

The internet and social media have made reading a much more interactive and collaborative experience. Readers can share passages they have enjoyed with other readers. Books take on a second life as they are discussed among fans and sometimes with the author on social media platforms. The author may answer questions and even make changes so that the story evolves into a conversation between the writer and readers.

Augmented reality. Augmented-reality (AR) books contain extra layers of content, which can be revealed by an app on a smartphone. This could be a video clip, audio commentary, game, or 3D projection. The primary market for AR today is in children's books. It can bring an adventure story to life with special sound effects, or display a 3D view of a planet in a book about space. Readers need only download the app. They hold their cellular device above a trigger, such as a QR code, for the AR content to appear. Another approach is to embed ultrathin solar panels within the leaves of a printed book. The panels generate electricity, which activates the book's AR content.

Print on demand. Traditional printing presses require large print runs to keep the costs of individual books low. Thanks to digital printing technology, it is now possible to print and bind a single book at a reasonable cost. This is good news for publishers hoping to avoid the cost of storing unsold books, and also for self-published authors who can print individual books to order. In the future, you may buy a book from a digital catalog at your local café and have it printed while you drink your coffee.

AI in publishing. AI tools can help publishers analyze the entire content of their backlist. It can identify what content can be reused and repackaged as new books and also show where there are content gaps. AI can spot factual inaccuracies, **plagiarism,** and breaches of copyright in manuscripts. It can provide translations and automate such tasks as formatting, proofreading, and grammar checking, giving editors more time to focus on the quality of the writing.

4 MOVIES

THE FUTURE OF FILM

Cinema is a relatively young art form and one that has always been driven by technological change. Such advances as green screens, CGI, and animation allowed filmmakers to make evermore spectacular movies. Today's technologies continue to push the limits of what is visually possible on screen. With the latest techniques, physical and digital elements seamlessly mesh with no need for a green screen. Aging actors can be made to look younger or be replaced altogether by digital lookalikes.

Technology is also helping to streamline the filmmaking process, making it less expensive and more accessible to those without the resources of a Hollywood studio. Filmmakers can plan their movies at a relatively low cost thanks to 3D previsualization and can produce their props with a computer and 3D printer. AI has become an integral part of the movie industry, helping directors, producers, casting agents, editors, and marketers in their work. Before long, we may be watching movies produced, directed, and written by an AI, and featuring robots as actors.

MAKING MOVIES

Today, we live in a new and dynamic era of cinema. Fantasy and action movies are becoming evermore visually striking. Filmmakers can achieve their visions on reasonable budgets and in good time thanks to rapid advances in an array of technologies, including cameras, computers, and 3D printing.

Cameras and drones. Modern films are shot on digital cameras that are small and lightweight compared to earlier cinema cameras. They have a high resolution, provide sharp images with fine detail, and can operate at up to 360 frames per second for slow-motion action scenes. **Drones** fixed with cameras allow filmmakers to capture aerial shots that were previously difficult or expensive. Modern AI drones can avoid obstacles and frame aerial shots with little need for human input from the ground.

3D previsualization. Traditionally, filmmakers planned a movie using storyboards—a sequence of drawings representing the scenes they wished to create. They would walk through a set before filming, *blocking* a scene (figuring out the actors' moves in relation to the camera) and making adjustments to the lighting, props, and scenery. It is a time-consuming and costly process. Today, with 3D previsualization software, a filmmaker can create a 3D digital replica of a movie set on a computer. This allows them to explore and experiment with different shots in their own time before setting foot on set. They can share their work with the cast and crew, so everyone knows what they have to do.

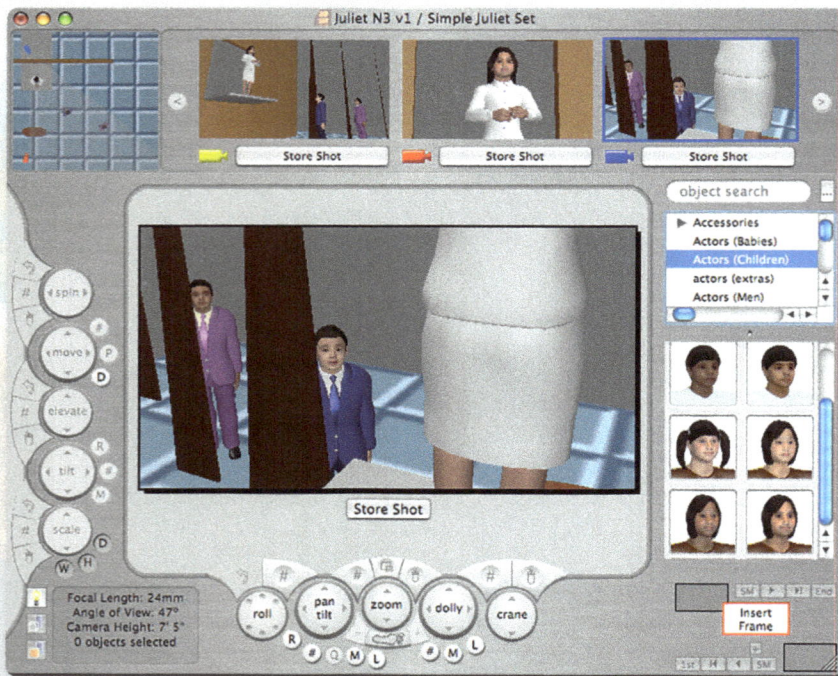

Juliet N3 v1 / Simple Juliet Set

Store Shot

Store Shot

Store Shot

object search

Accessories
Actors (Babies)
Actors (Children)
actors (extras)
Actors (Men)

Store Shot

Focal Length: 24mm
Angle of View: 47°
Camera Height: 7' 5"
0 objects selected

spin
move
elevate
tilt
scale

roll
pan tilt
zoom
dolly
crane

Insert Frame

3D-printed props. Movie props are now designed and created in hours instead of days thanks to 3D printing. To make a prop, a model is designed on a computer or scanned from a physical object, then saved as a digital file before being printed. 3D printed props are highly accurate, realistic, and detailed. Different versions can be tested with small adjustments made to the digital file.

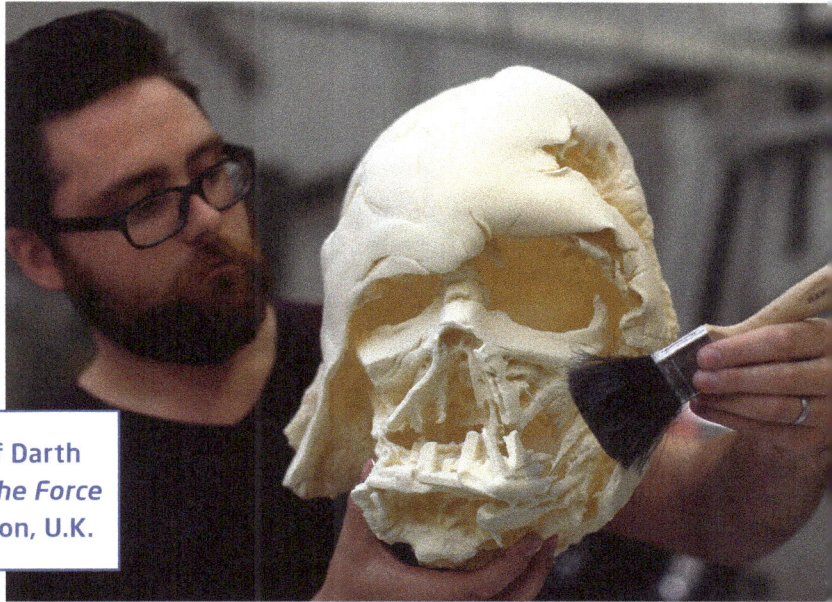

A technician holds a 3D-printed replica of Darth Vader's melted helmet from *Star Wars: The Force Awakens* at Pinewood Studios near London, U.K.

The Volume. Today, blockbuster movies are shot using a new technology known as the Volume. This is a circular studio with walls made up of large LED panels. The screens display the background of the scene in perfect clarity, whether it is an alien landscape or a spaceship. The LED screens are "smart," so they respond to the movement of the camera by adjusting perspective, lighting, and other elements in real time. For the actors, this is easier than working with a green screen because they can interact with the world around them and don't have to imagine what they are seeing.

AI AND ACTORS

Today, we can no longer be sure that the actors we see in films look anything like the characters they portray. They may have been digitally altered to look older, younger, fatter, or thinner. They may not exist at all. For filmmakers, it is convenient to work with virtual or digitally reconstructed actors. Their performances can be tweaked repeatedly, and they are always available for reshoots. But is this fair to actors? And how do audience members feel about this?

Digital recreation. Today, it is possible to digitally recreate actors who have died or to "de-age" older actors so they appear as their younger selves. First, a look-alike is filmed performing the necessary actions. Computer-generated imagery then inserts the actor's face. Actors have their faces scanned in an illumination system named the Light Stage. Surrounded by more than 10,000 LED's, the actor makes up to 50 different facial expressions. With each expression, the actor is lit and photographed from all angles. An AI algorithm uses this data to digitally superimpose their face into any movie scene. The technology faithfully reproduces the color and texture of the actor's skin in all lighting conditions.

Virtual actors. Filmmakers are increasingly making use of computer-generated virtual actors. Virtual actors are sometimes used as "digital doubles" of real actors. A digital double can perform dangerous stunts or act in environments that would be risky for humans. Such doubles can be created through motion capture, which records the performance of a real actor. Only the movements of the actor are recorded, not the appearance. This data is then mapped onto a 3D model of the virtual actor so that it can perform the same actions.

Robot actors. We are some way from a world in which human actors must compete for roles with robots. However, one robot has already taken the first step in that direction. Erica is the star of a science-fiction movie, *b*. Created for the role by Japanese scientists Hiroshi Ishiguro and Kohei Ogawa, she had to be taught how to act. Memorizing lines wasn't a problem, but learning how to say them with emotion, and how to move her body naturally, was more of a challenge.

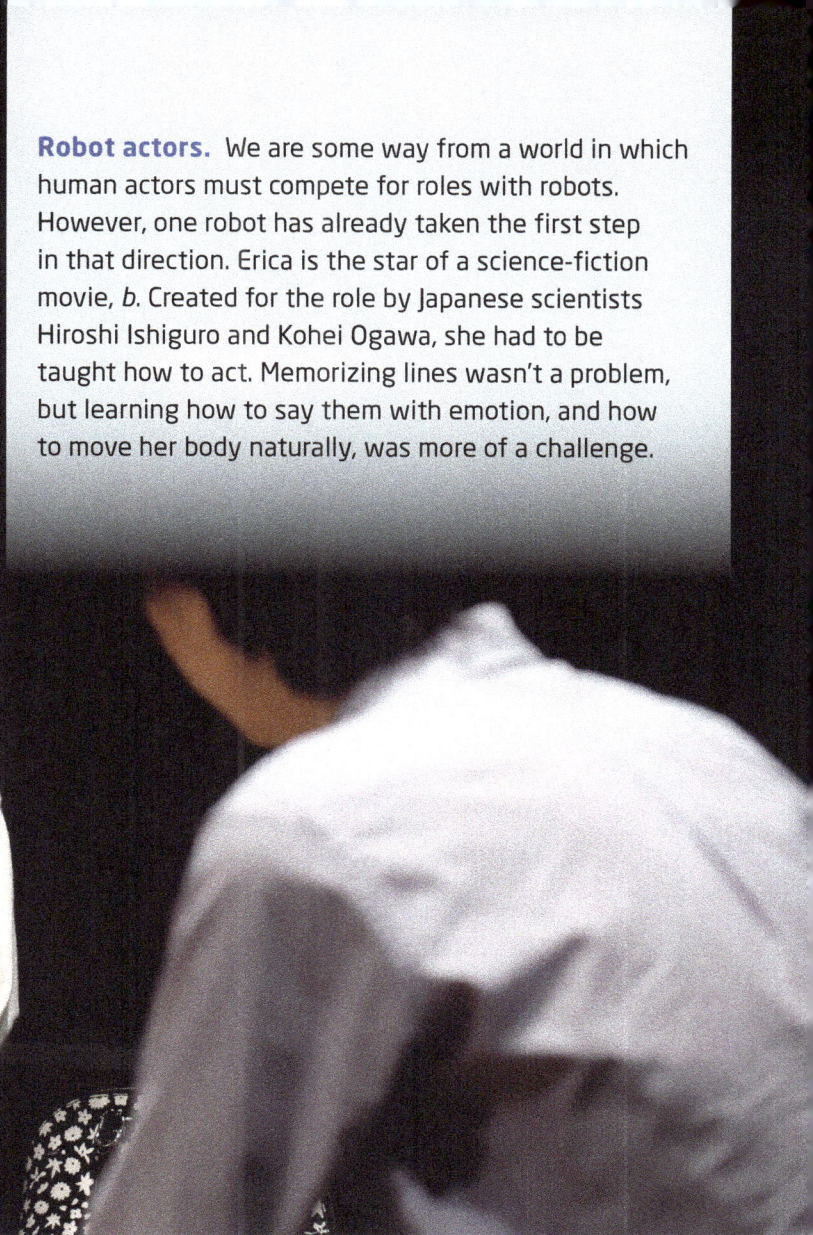

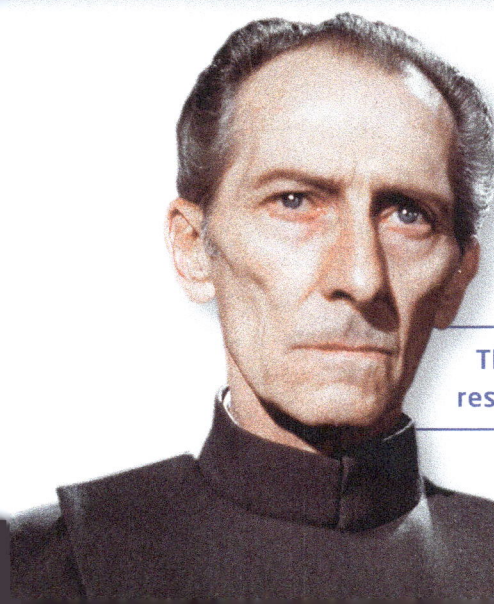

Is it fair for dead actors to be digitally resurrected when they cannot give permission? Should living actors have control over their virtual doubles? What if these digital clones are made to say or do things the actor disagrees with? Will human actors get fewer roles if their clone can be used more cheaply? Many people working as extras in the film industry are already losing jobs because filmmakers are using virtual actors for crowd scenes.

The actor Peter Cushing, who died in 1994, was digitally resurrected for the 2016 movie *Rogue One: A Star Wars Story.*

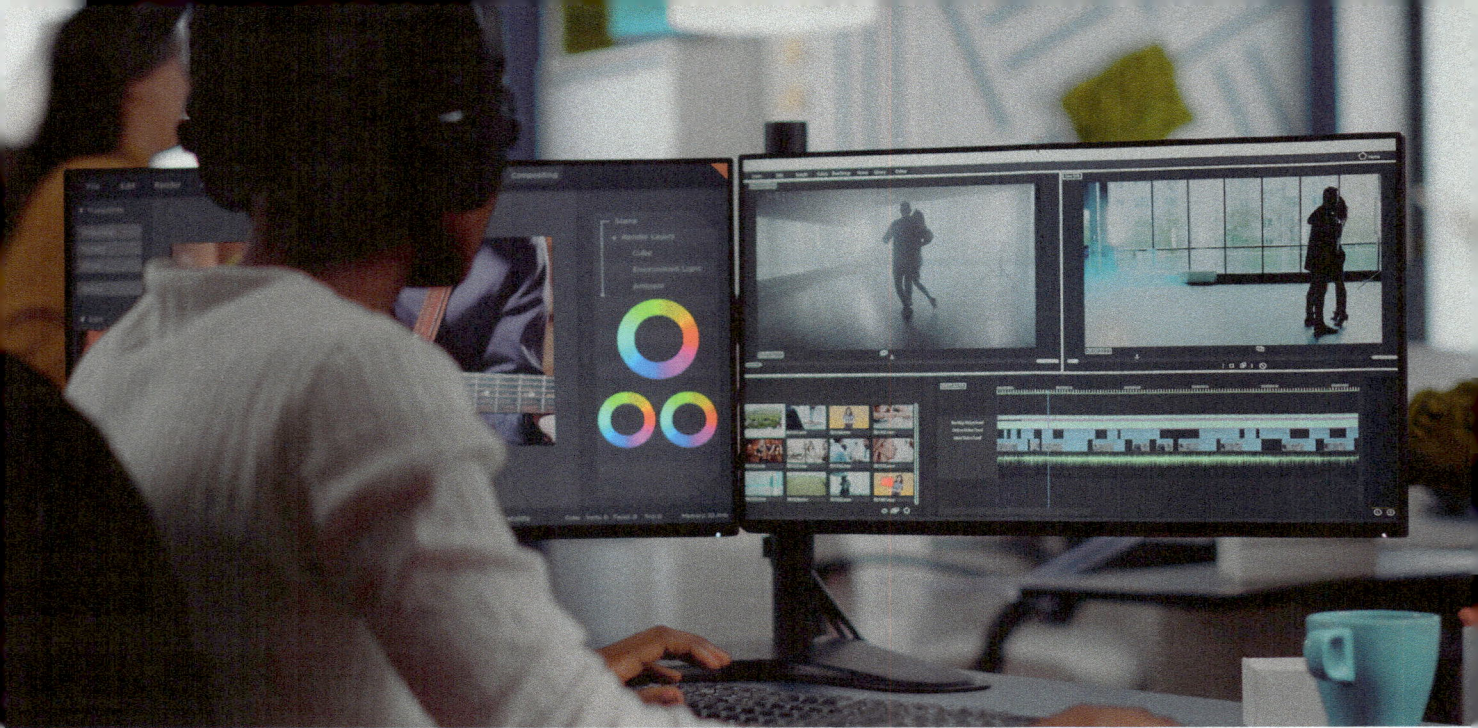

AI AND MOVIE EDITING

Today, artificial intelligence is playing an increasingly important role in the postproduction phase of moviemaking. Once a movie has been shot, the director and the film editor work on the footage, cutting and editing it to create the finished movie.

Algorithmic editing. AI is helping to automate and streamline film editing. Thanks to facial recognition technology, algorithms can recognize characters and identify the scenes where they appear. The algorithms can be programmed to perform simple editing tasks, such as switching to a different camera perspective after a set number of frames. One day, computers may even learn how to apply editing techniques to create tension or add drama.

Changing dialogue. It is not uncommon for actors to mess up or forget a line of dialogue. This may only be noticed after the fact, requiring expensive reshoots. An algorithm developed at Stanford University promises to make editing dialogue as easy as text editing. It allows an editor to modify a scene using a text transcript of the dialogue. If the actor misspeaks, the editor can delete the unwanted words and type in the correct ones. The algorithm then extracts the speech sounds and lip movements for the new words from elsewhere in the video and pastes these into the film. The program smoothes and synchronizes the speech to look and sound natural to the viewer.

Sound editing. An important part of film editing is the addition of sound effects. These could be weather sounds, traffic noise, footsteps, or explosions. The latest AI algorithms can recognize the action on the screen and automatically insert the appropriate sound effects, synchronizing them perfectly with the images.

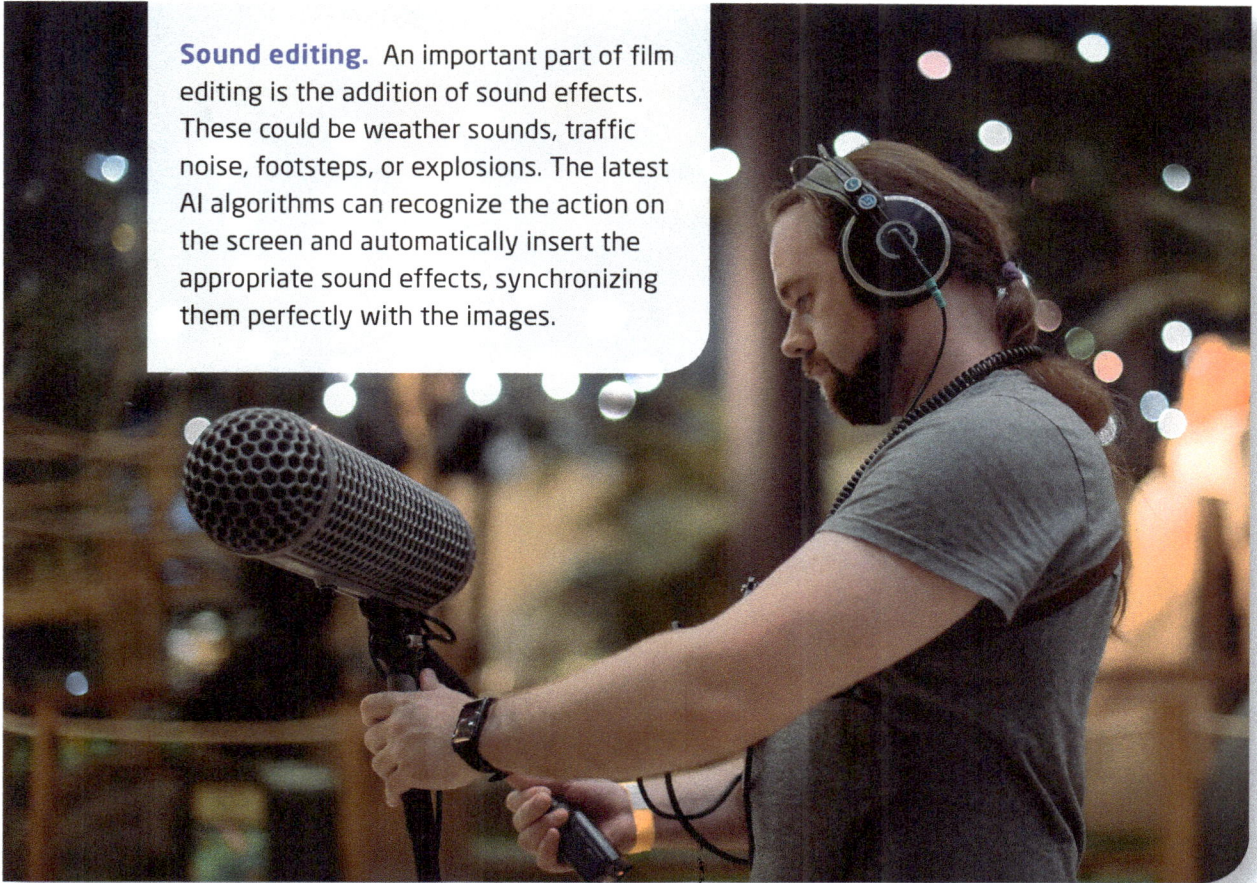

Dubbing. Dubbed films can look weird when lip movements do not match the words spoken. A U.K.-based technology company named Flawless AI has solved this problem. They use AI to digitally alter video so that an actor's lips match the voice actor's words on the audio track. Another problem with dubbed films is that the voice doesn't always suit the actor. Israel-based company Deepdub can fix that. Its AI can make the dubbed voice sound exactly like that of the original actor. All it needs is a two-minute sample of the actor's voice, and it can synthesize a soundalike voice to say the actor's lines in any language.

AI AND THE BOX OFFICE

Movies are big financial investments, and film studios will do everything they can to make them popular and successful. Once they relied on experience, gut instinct, and test screenings. These days, studios are increasingly turning to AI to help boost a film's chances of success at the box office.

Analyzing scripts. Film studios are using AI to figure out which movies will have the maximum appeal. One company, ScriptBook, uses a machine-learning system to analyze film scripts and determine their likely success based on data from over six thousand previous movie scripts. The AI reports on the target audience, points out potential flaws, and predicts a film's likely box office revenue.

Market-analyzing actors. Casting movies is a high-risk business. Getting the right actor for the main role can be the difference between success or failure at the box office. An AI program named Cinelytic looks at how movies have performed and cross-references this with information about the movies' themes and actors. The AI uses this data to predict how a new movie will perform at the box office with a particular actor. It can even break down the appeal of particular actors across different segments of the population or different regions.

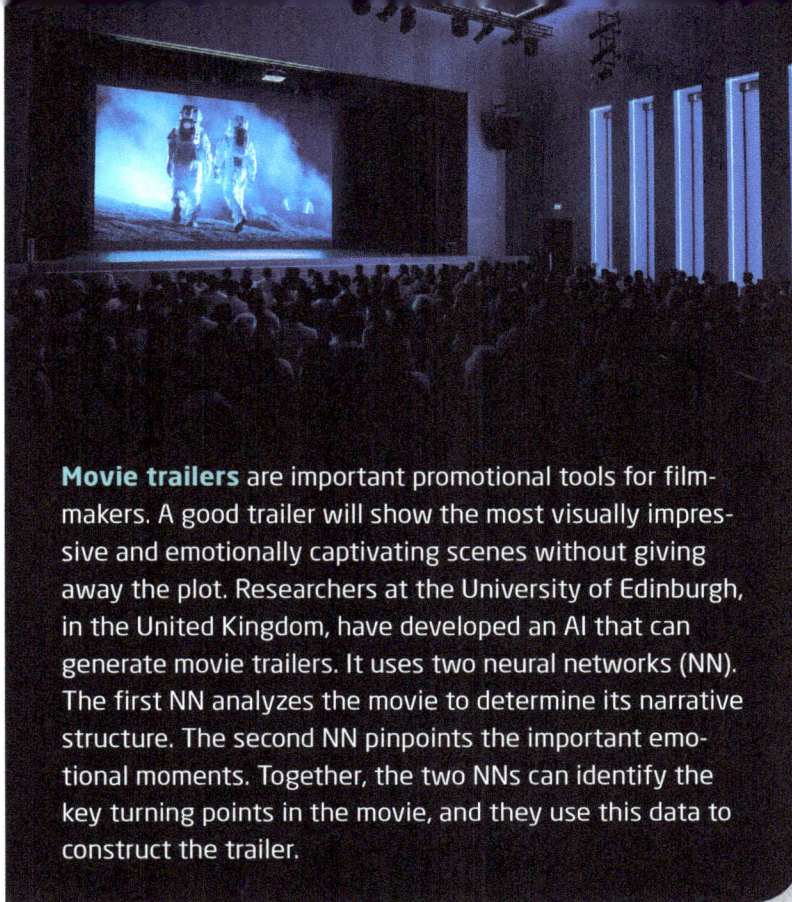

Movie trailers are important promotional tools for film-makers. A good trailer will show the most visually impressive and emotionally captivating scenes without giving away the plot. Researchers at the University of Edinburgh, in the United Kingdom, have developed an AI that can generate movie trailers. It uses two neural networks (NN). The first NN analyzes the movie to determine its narrative structure. The second NN pinpoints the important emotional moments. Together, the two NNs can identify the key turning points in the movie, and they use this data to construct the trailer.

The downside. The financial risks involved to produce a movie make it understandable that film studios will seek support from AI. The risk is that an overreliance on AI will lead to movies that look and sound quite similar. AI relies on data from past films to generate its recommendations. This makes it less good at predicting changes in audience tastes. Some films that performed poorly when they were released proved culturally influential later on. For example, the film *Citizen Kane* was a box office failure. But it is now regarded as one of the greatest ever movies. If an AI had been consulted at the time, this film might never have been made.

Blade Runner (1982) was not a financial success when it was released but is now considered a sci-fi classic.

THE CINEMA EXPERIENCE

Thanks to the rise of streaming giants such as Netflix and Amazon Prime, television is experiencing a golden age. Cinemas must work harder to compete, and one way of doing so is through technology. Some of today's cinemas offer new sensory experiences that are not yet available on television along with top-quality pictures and sound.

Screen X movie theaters offer a 270-degree viewing experience using side walls so the audience feels fully immersed in the movie. Whereas most cinemas use one projector, Screen X theaters use five—one for the main screen and four for the side walls. Computer software blends these images to create a uniform effect so that the action appears to extend straight out of the screen. Movies intended for Screen X are typically shot with three cameras to provide content for projection on the side walls.

4DX film tech in cinema goes beyond sight and sound. This technology incorporates other senses to draw us closer to the world of the movie. Seats roll, sway, heave, and shake in synch with the action on the screen. Legs and necks are tickled. Audiences can feel the wind and rain in their faces and the vibrations of a motorcycle as if they're actually riding. The air is scented, water sprays, smoke billows, strobe lights flash, and simulated snow may fall. Theaters even provide haptic vests so audiences can feel the impact of punches in fight scenes.

AR and VR. Augmented reality overlays digital elements on the physical world, while virtual reality immerses the viewer in a virtual world. Both will have profound effects on how movies are made and experienced. You could don your AR glasses and see 3D characters emerge from the screen, or a planet suspended in the air above you. Or you could call up the backstory of a character and have it superimposed on the screen for reference.

With your VR headset, you could wander around inside the world of the movie, observing the scenes from different angles and even trying out different storylines. For this, filmmakers need to shoot multiple perspectives in the same movie and explore several different plot twists. You could watch the same movie repeatedly and have a different ending each time. The viewer could interact with and even be a character in the movie via an avatar. It would hand control of the story from the filmmaker to the viewer. Some see this as an evolution of storytelling, calling it "storyliving."

The opening of the world's first VR movie cinema, at the 20th China Beijing International High-Tech Expo (CHITEC), in Beijing, June 2017

ENGAGE YOUR READER

Nonfiction writing often includes subject-specific vocabulary terms. Knowing the words related to the topic helps us understand the text itself.

When good readers come upon words they don't know well, they pause and try to figure them out. One tool they use is the glossary, like the one on page 4. Not every word can be defined in a glossary, though!

Authors know this, so they leave clues about words in the text. Next time you encounter a challenging word, stop and look for information about its meaning in the surrounding sentences. Sometimes authors define the term right there in the text! Other times, they'll compare the term to something you may already know. Authors even use punctuation like commas or dashes to clue you in to a word's meaning.

INSTRUCTIONS

1. Consider the list of challenge words and identify where each is used in the text. You can use the Index on page 48 to help you locate each term.

2. Explain how the author described each word. Ask yourself "what is happening in the text?" or "how is this word being used?" as you search for clues about their meanings.

3. Create your own definitions of the words. Don't just copy the dictionary definitions. Instead think about how you would tell a friend what each term means.

4. Add a visual representation for each word. Think about what you could draw that will help you remember what the words mean.

CHALLENGE WORDS

- Artificial intelligence (AI)
- Holography
- Algorithm
- Neural network (NN)

- Generative adversarial networks (GAN)
- Machine learning
- Copyright
- Augmented reality (AR)

EXAMPLE

Challenge Word	Page(s)	Author's Description	Personal Definition	Visual Representation
Artificial intelligence (AI)	5	- the ability of a computer system to process information like human thought or to exhibit human behavior -this technology collaborates with artists to produce work	Technology that tries to mimic human thoughts and actions. It is gaining in popularity and use in such fields as the arts, music, writing, and film	
Holography				

INDEX

www.ingramcontent.com/pod-product-compliance
Lightning Source LLC
Chambersburg PA
CBHW061420090426
42744CB00018B/2075